that's what you get

Also by Sheila Maldonado

one-bedroom solo

that's what you get

Sheila Maldonado

Brooklyn Arts Press • New York

that's what you get
© 2021 Sheila Maldonado

ISBN-13: 978-1-936767-59-5

Cover and interior design by Shanna Compton. Edited by Joe Pan.
Author photo by Nikki Johnson.

Published in the United States of America by:
Brooklyn Arts Press
154 N 9th St #1
Brooklyn, NY 11249
www.BrooklynArtsPress.com
info@BrooklynArtsPress.com

Distributed to the trade by Small Press Distribution / SPD

Library of Congress Cataloging-in-Publication Data:

Names: Maldonado, Sheila, author.
Title: That's what you get : (poems) / Sheila Maldonado.
Description: First edition. | Brooklyn, NY : Brooklyn Arts Press, [2021] |
    Summary: "The second collection of poetry by Sheila Maldonado"--
    Provided by publisher.
Identifiers: LCCN 2020017507 | ISBN 9781936767595 (paperback)
Subjects: LCGFT: Poetry.
Classification: LCC PS3613.A435224 T47 2020 | DDC 811/.6--dc23
LC record available at https://lccn.loc.gov/2020017507

First Edition

Para Mami,
Vilma Maldonado

I'm not good or real. I'm evil and imaginary.
—Karen Walker, *Will & Grace*

Contents

showing papers II: long form blackout

for the brown dreamers and the black president
who turned in their documents

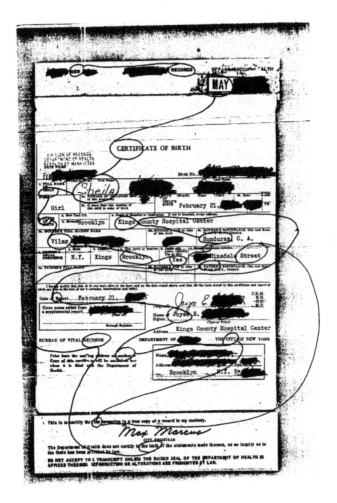

New records may certifi Sheila
child of Vilma Brooklyn yes
and Honduras kings
Re Joyce mother city
the street father records the truth

poet in a shade of jade

I am so jealous of how poor you are
of how you are poor
your particular stilo pobre
The way you put no cash and
no money together is uncanny
This aesthetic
lack of change combined
with lack of dollars
is very difficult to duplicate
and I hate you for that

I was gonna go hear you read
from your new collection of
unpaid bills
just the other day
but you get readings
all the time
you have your pick
of not being paid
or being unpaid
You get to ride
the subway back and forth
on your own dime
and you buy your
performance alcohol

I'll make it one of these days
give you dirty looks
as you read and rake in
your air bucks

What I look forward to most
is not tolerating
how you hoard your poverty
tell no one your secret
you must have some malefactor
mentor
mentiroso
who further mystifies
the acquisition of wealth
and points you in the direction
of the dead end

Emersonian fashion advice

there is still a chill
in all the large bodies
of the city
man-made and natural

the surrounding waters
the thickets of tree and bush
the subway platforms
all holding onto cold

the season
in the midst of its turn

therefore recognize
it is not
open-toe time yet
not the moment
for booty shorts

heed this call not
in the name of
slut shame
but cold awareness

carry some socks
a pair of leggings
a sweater
be prudent
young exhibitionist

I grant you
climate change
does make choice difficult
but when in doubt
err on the side of warmth

otherwise
your wait for the express
will be extra nippy
your hang in the park
will turn quickly with the light
your walk by the river
will surprise with its bite

understand what it is
to read the day
to be cozy and
right with yourself
the environment
and its weather

live in the reality of
temperature

let the season unfold
give it its time
yes the winter was harsh
but this city
doesn't ever warm up
till at least May

epic laundry

a former nonprofit staffer
turned real estate agent tells me
laundry is too political
he sends it out now
he can afford to

I am still in the laundry struggle
the managing of the cloth
the managing of the time
it takes to manage the cloth
the hard labor of the destitute

heavy lifting and carting
into a top floor elevator
out the door to the street
home washer/dryers
the stuff of TV fantasy

at the laundromat I am confused
for the worker women
in my uniform of invisibility
braless in an old dark t-shirt
and high-water sweats

hair pulled back strays flying loose
my robust skin of servitude
the washerwoman by a river
scraping rags on a board
changing your dollar for quarters

I don't have any on me
I don't know what is wrong
with the machine
don't ask me what I charge
by the pound

I have my own epic laundry
like debt weeks of neglect
panty shortages and crises
all the holey t-shirts
that must be preserved

I am here for my zen penance
my workout in the back sweating
deep in the dryer heat
headphones on dancing
as I manipulate my rags

one owner admiring my zeal
showed me her tricks
pulled me and my fitted bedsheet
out onto the tiled floor
drawing me into her secret fold

I have since betrayed her
with a facility closer to my home
my burden too great to wheel
three extra blocks forsaking
communion for convenience

there I wash and fold with true
toilers nonowners fabric slaves
loveless and rightfully so
we share no confidences
only questions like complaints

my devotion to repetition
precision creases
organized by roy g biv
all underground all unnoticed
my order private

stop asking me to do yours

submit / resist

submit to the line of students as questions
resist their tall tales
submit to the stage of the classroom
resist the despair of unpreparedness
the blank stares blank papers
submit to the penal scholastic
resist the hourly rage
submit time sheet essay humility
resist the conspiratorial bank
remit subsist
submit to the clutch of the breast
resist the song of the uterus
submit to the will of the crotch
to the ass jet to the bike seat
resist memory failure humidity
submit to the one breeze
resist gerunds
submit to the peripathetic
resist the howl of the building don
submit to the raindrops on the air conditioner
resist the caffeine tremor
submit to the sweat lodge
resist the butter cookie
submit to the butter cookie
resist the baby squeal behind the neighbor door
submit to architecture and its facades
resist gatekeepers
submit to disorientation
to starting over and again

smoke ring

that's what you get
for thinking a vaporizer was an engagement ring
he wasn't on his knees he was opening his car trunk
that wasn't a ribbon undone that was a black plastic bag
that sapphire wasn't a rock it was a shaft
those weren't vows that was vapor
that wasn't vapor that was smoke
a bill of smoke a ring of goods
a haze a daze a mirror
what he wanted you to see
what you get for believing
that wasn't a promise that was a cough

ode to the mammogram

ah mzungu
maker of ingenious contraptions
I would have loved to be
at the medical expo where
this machine was introduced
the boardroom
the office
where it was pitched
pioneers introducing
the chest compressor x-ray

no one prepared me for this rite
no one said that after 40
a robot not unlike the one
Sigourney Weaver worked
at the end of *Aliens*
will come for your boob
and squeeze it flat
with its giant metal pincers

it needs a cohort
to help it get a grip
on your mammary
a technician trying
to wrangle it
onto the glass
like Mix-a-Lot
floppy and shifty
like catching a jellyfish

she was trying to get
a nipple profile
she said
and we all danced
an awkward dance
the teat technician
and me
the breast
and the machine

I felt for the
little titty ladies
I thought mine
were hard to tame
but those women
must suffer more
must feel
the pinch worse

the assistant to the
bosom compressor
soldiers on
regardless of size
she cannot laugh
the joke is old
the girls are old
that's all you get
on that job

me
I can't be taken anywhere
I am an awkward boy
who can't deal with her aging
I am sure the compressor

has saved many lives
don't mean to mock
its usefulness
but still am shocked
I must discover
this all for myself
no warning
there is no brochure
for immature tomboys
new to this side of life
the take-care-of-yourself
all-you-have-
is-your-health side
women's medicine
stays a new field
to fools

my-kus

illiteracy

contagious
insanity

a secret incest
like incest

internal
shame

make
it a joy

my rage

not righteous
like Malcolm
irrational like
hammer-wielding dude
in the street

how to make the Heights Coney Island

get a bike
ride down the hills

boom
roller coaster

I'm so native

I'm alien

pluma

felt tip rolling ball
scratchy smooth
I'm only in writing
for the pens

temporary statement

I am not poignant. I am losing nuance. I beat you over the head. I am cliché. I am a caveman. Cavewoman. A cave. I am not genteel or radical. I am pissed. I am not always specific. I am beat. I am losing steam. I leave image with image and word with word. I take too many pictures. I am literal as fuck. I bully my way through a text. I barrel my way through. That Neanderthal thing again. I resist understanding. I understand cuz I resist. I've forgotten how to break a line. The line breaks me. I use I too much. I do get that the I on the page is still not me. I do get that. I don't know if you get that. I don't know who I am in this time. I have lost a great love. I am suffering a terrible leader. I don't know where to turn or who to be. I am looking for my days to reacquire some rhythm. I can't be kind in the morning. I can't be kind. I am mourning. I miss touch. I miss conversations I had in the past. I miss the conversation I had with my past. It is leaving me. I don't mind erasing. I want to know who to address though.

showing papers I: pregnant while brown

after the laws of Arizona 2012

I was pregnant with a book a brown book
every month pregnant every month brown
birthing documents long forms short stories
hidden histories tall tales tongue twisters
pregnant every month a bloody flight
from two Nogaleses pregnant
with a bloody book on the brown side
of history in the arid Spanish
native land ink expelled blood erased
pregnant every month with unwanted words
wrapped in a certificate abandoned
womb text a border infiltrated
pages smuggled crumpled bleeding brown
history a fugitive in the womb

peluche perdido plushie lost

Disney Central Americans in Times Square

there's an Elmo on the beast
fuzzy red blurry
atop the train
traversing Middle-earth

he's coming north
for a smile a buck
what was taken
what was promised

you fear he will fondle
your child in the
crossroads
of the clock

elmolestor
U.S.-abused
peripherally addled
by animation
and supremacies

he's with Minnie
her bow fluttering
in the train whoosh
disk eyes aloft
pink cuticle shoes
bound to black feet

she removes
her head

wears it cocked
on an indigenous crown

hot day on the square
she fumbles through
her drawstring knapsack
for a water bottle

detaches the native skull
sits it atop the
mini Minnie within

and still I lay

(forgive me Ms. Angelou
who was An-gel-low not -loo
as I say lay not lie)

I place me on the couch like this
I am up on the sofa that way
like Usain Bolt horizontal
a champion of lay

without an object or a past
you may say the word is lie
but I lay as nothingness complete
time and substance don't apply

I'm getting old and had a hole
bored into my right hip
it changed my laying style
and I am stronger for it

I put the lay in lazy
how lazy do you say
too much to keep up this rhyme
pardon me as I stray

because with every passing day
I am asked to play mother teacher
representative of race
I lay

because I am more often
the representative
of running away
I lay

because it is assumed
I was raised on
tortillas and dirt
I lay

that would be my mom
you would want to speak to her
so that she may slap you
upside the head with her eyes
from the queen-size bed
in which she lays

she worked on a
banana plantation
in a lamp factory
and drove
a mini school bus
so that she could lay

I do the lord's work
teaching students
with nothing
having nothing myself
so I lay

no one pays me
to grade all these
damn papers

all the damn time
I am laying

I have no children
and still get so many
tossed upon me
as I lay

you can watch
the whole world
implode from your couch
if you lay

when one finds oneself
in the tropics
one uses a hammock
to lay

action is better
than laying yes
but laying is better
than panicking
lay

if I'm not
at every march
that is OK
I've been
in those streets
I've walked for you
why don't you
walk for me
while I lay

if you would rather
call it self-care
that Audre thought
was self-preservation
was warfare
then wage war
and lay

"Remain useless
unmoving till
the action is right"
said Lao Tzu
which meant
lay too

there is truth
in the sedentary
strategy
in the cut
in which
you may lay

"In America
I was free only
in battle
never free to rest
and he who finds
no way to rest
cannot long
survive the battle"

said Baldwin
from his bed
to paraphrase

he meant
if you wanna stay
you should lay some

he too might
have been
laying low
from a virus
of which too many
had to be convinced

he was exhausted
from constantly relaying
this message
Professor Broken Record
he had to lay
from all the relaying

they all kept saying
your xenophobia
and productivity
are gonna kill you
lay

when you tell me
write 'resist'
what I read 'is rest'
and lay

because my exhaustion
has grown deeper
than my rage
I lay
I lay
I lay

Garner verdict night (Dec 3 2014)

for Monica Hand

1. meeting the march at 50th and Broadway

dropped grading papers
soon as I heard, I had more
to teach by walking

marching was mourning
I felt I knew him, neighbors
from remote ghettos

like someone I grew
up with, surrounded by white
ethnics in the sticks

his video ghost
told me there was no question
I had to be there

2. sit-in at Columbus Circle

we sat down in a
crosswalk, Christmas lights of the
luxury mall winking

this couldn't be done
under Bloomberg, he corralled
blocked, barricaded

had people believing
they had to ask permission
to protest, to breathe

never felt more of this
city than when I took
my place on that road

3. between the buses down 9th

against traffic down
wide Manhattan avenue
eyes in back of our heads

many marchers the
age of my students, I fell
back to watch them move

was solo among
groups of various sizes
could observe weave join

break, let one know where
the other was, if they were
lost, coming apart

4. flag on West Side Highway

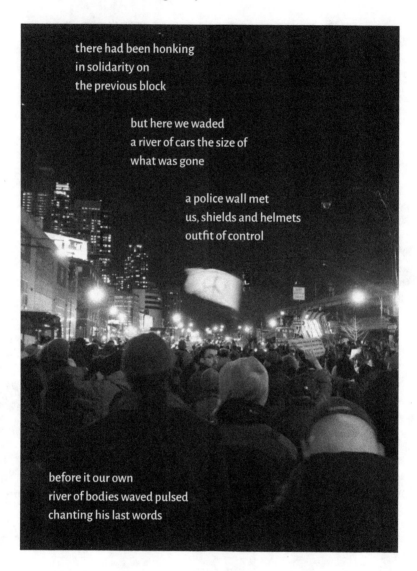

there had been honking
in solidarity on
the previous block

but here we waded
a river of cars the size of
what was gone

a police wall met
us, shields and helmets
outfit of control

before it our own
river of bodies waved pulsed
chanting his last words

my-kus

sacrifice

I wanna cut
my heart out
of my chest
be my
own offering

also ran out
of green tea

spectrum

I'm not all of the gay
that likes all of the people
I am some of the gay
that likes some of the people

fuckin pantheon

I banish you
to my imagination
all of you
figments
of my masturbation

last of the Mandos

I came to the family
surly and sick
on the Sunday visit

so my father
so Mando
before my mother
Woman
recognize my plight

She was saying
she had no food ready
I rolled my eyes
and sucked my teeth
like him

Ralph Kramden
Mando Kramden
a Brooklyn baby
angry at mama
I hacked disgust

of course
she had some
leftover pork chops
that were still good

She was all
they were better
yesterday

when you were
supposed to come

pero estaba mal
de veras mal*

*but I wasn't well
really not well

In illness I can be Pa
the-world-owes-me Pa
especially my wife
my mama

they owe me for
making me stick around
I could just as easily go
disappear

disappearing comes easy
to our bloodline

you want me here
gimme some grub
you don't
let me wither
in my woe

Ma still responds
she wants me to be
Mando in the flesh
the last reflection of him
cagadita a el**

**exactly like him (as if he shitted me out)

she is soft
mansita
a Taurus tame

answering
the Leo father
in me

she remembers
the wounded lion roar

She worries about me
when I leave
don't fall asleep
on the train

I always tell her
they're afraid of me
I'm the mugger

daughter of a man
confused for mugger
a man who played one

I once caught him
on the train
at one end of a car
disheveled

one pant leg tucked in
the other hanging out
of his Velcro sneakers

his button-down
undone and sloppy
over his sagging slacks

eyes bugged out
wide wild
like a *Thriller* zombie

don't fuck with me
leaning up
on the silver doors

¿Pa?

when he saw me
he snapped
out of posture
uno se tiene
que hacer el loco***   ***one has to play the crazy

In madness I am Pa
feigned crazy
that becomes real

protection from
true psychos
faking better

no se preocupa Ma****   ****don't worry Ma
I'm very Pa today

blood to the hospital

mother
        (solitude) blood
    hospital

            father

            darkness
in the middle

mother   night

    spitting

dad dad dad

sangre al hospital

madre en la soledad
escupiendo sangre
soledad mas madre
en el hospital

soledad mas sola
no la hacen ni madre
en el hospital
donde murió padre
–dad –dad –dad

madre en la oscuridad
al hospital de padre
en medio de la noche
sangre al hospital

madre en la noche
al hospital de sangre
escupiendo padre
en la oscuridad
–dad –dad –dad

Ma's Palm Sunday TV (*María* vs. *Nuestra Belleza Latina*)

All the baby boys in Bethlehem slaughtered
Mary and Joseph getting away with baby Jesus on a donkey
Flip
Beauties in spokesmodel competition brutalizing banter
making asses of themselves
Flip
Jesus all grown already turning water to wine
proud mama Mary looking on
Flip
Contestants as future video whores winding their bodies
around Daddy Yankee
Flip
Joseph near death after fainting on a carpentry job
Our Lady at his bedside
Flip
Our non-virgins as actresses dying onstage
saviorless
Flip
Salome writhing before Herod
and rewarded with whatsoever she desires
her mother telling her to ask for John the Baptist's head
Mary Magdalene running out screaming Noooo
Flip
Aflac commercial
The duck is in the hospital
Flip
Same commercial
Flip
A belleza standing before the judges
made to address her nude Twitter pix

I did not consent that is my private life
it does not affect my dignity as a woman
Flip
Mary Magdalene bent before a circle of men with rocks in hand
Jesus stepping in with his line about sin and the first stone

my-kus

Koni Ailan

sleepy oven pork
seagull lampposts
nursing home projects

niece blanketed with dolls
our voices
Ma's chanclas clicking
in the hallway

Samaritan

When someone is outside the turnstile waving their wrist asking for a swipe,
I am often ready to help out with my unlimited MetroCard as I exit the station,
cuz that is just the kind of person I am, thinking of others.

Brooklyn

really betrays you
don't tell me you're fuckin from there
till you get kicked out

I'm not

human and universal
I'm alien and local

41

child to her pop

I stay watching the '80s fail, the '80s art fail, the pop fall apart. I see the joy destroyed, don't want to blame the drugs, want to blame the people, blame society. the eating of the black celebrity. what did you do to Michael. what did you do to the child watching Michael. black pop joy, a mirage. as good as any. better. as American as any. more. some were too good to be good, too true to be true. the work what speaks for them but then there are children, then there are victims. art victims, pop victims. a child not artwork. a child, not product. a song, an episode, surviving a child. here we are art survivors, pop survivors. a regime of joy crumbling. missing our leaders. video as consolation. memory restored sacred. victims as remakes. narrative threats. return to the making it ok. I am a citizen of making it ok.

drop day

today a day of
drowning and dying
in post-nasal drip
and dominican drake
post-nasal drake
dominican drip
a day delirious
and drizzy
a drizzle of drizzy
drowning me
drowsy from
drug interactions
drake interactions
dextromethorphan
and drake
dominican drowsy
in post-racial drip
drowning
in dream
dropping
in dizzy
drip
drake
drip

meeting for worship (the night Björk DJ'ed in BK)

for GH

My lady the muse
who makes sun rays
of strobe lights

attracts
an overlooked demographic
Quakers of Central American descent

I came late
to get into her very exclusive set
line wrapping up the block

for a tiny club
but it turned out
I had people there

A high school mate
the tenth one
from the door

We were not close
but were kindred long ago
in a Quaker day school

She Guatemalan
Me Honduran
outliers in a Caribbean borough

therefore
fans of
Icelandic dance queens

Our muse
is a shaman witch
from a land

of no singing
banned by
Danish conquerors

why she chant-sings
almost spoken word
in her delivery

on line
my new old Friend
told me Guatemala

was a land of no dancing
frowned upon
like *Footloose*

frowning
the remnants
of conquest

_____

We showed up for
our sister representative of volcanos
of shaky ground like our sliver

of arts erased by conquerors
apocalypses
the weather

there to praise
and tremble
before her

erupt
reduce to rubble
remake

all we have is our devotion
how we earn our spots
on the floor

identify
who is from a silence
and explode

notes on *Dark Blood* (River Phoenix's last movie)

River Phoenix's last role was as a ⅛th Native American who did not have a name. He was Boy. His hair was black but his eyes still blue. He was very skinny.

He died with about 11 days left on the film. The director remembered him as very gentle. He wanted to talk about the movie's story in the Q&A after the screening but the story was River.

There were a bunch of Native Americans in the movie. The only non-Native American playing a Native American was River. It was set in New Mexico.

It started with the Anasazi. Those ruins that are a city in a canyon.
That might be Colorado. It starts there. You know there's gonna be trouble.
The lead lady drinks a Bud and then strips a shoulder for a picture in front of the ruins. Vulgarity before the ancient. The lady is the cause of all the trouble.

There was a very well cast dog or dogs that had a significant part or parts in it.

The director narrates major gaps in the film. It is incomplete. The movie pauses on a scene, sometimes goes black and we hear the director's voice. It is cheesy yet eerie. Time stopping. Holes like the desert landscape where it is set.
Like River leaving.

The director smuggled some parts of the film from one country to another.
He didn't touch it for 10 solid years from 1999–2009.

River died in 1993. I was studying abroad in Brazil. Brazil cried with me.
Milton Nascimento, one of their biggest singers, was as big a fan as I was.
He wrote a song to him years before.

Such a spoiler now, it must be spoiled, because it is spoiled, we know it is spoiled.

River's character dies in the movie. We see a death scene. We see him act out his death weeks before he actually dies. It is all of a sudden in the fragmented movie. As all of a sudden as it was for all of us.

There are times River gives Keanu in his delivery and then later Joaquin. The dark phoenix lived. The dark one plays dark very well. Sad country singer, mean pop star, jealous Caesar. The light phoenix died when he played dark.

Is it phoenixes? Phoenices? Is that where Phoenician comes from? There is no plural of phoenix. One dies and another rises from the ashes. There can only be one at a time.

my-kus

Honduras poems tk

first and last of my line
there are no generations of me

Coney alien

I'm so Native American
I'm Asian

I'm so ahead of my time
I don't exist

barbecue

biking past all the families grilling
don't really want the families
just really want the meat

mite b ur hi priestess tho

have no advice for u
I am not ur mother
or ur guru priest

winter zuihitsu

my vagina was your death therapist

city of villains and failures

some days I can't take my hardline friends
they can't handle my inability to draw a line

did stop writing at least once to check phone
like I'm on call for a job I don't have

there is survival of a genocide in the blood memory
does that make us as afloat as we are today
I don't know but there is something essentially crappy

today I'm focusing on the forms
I'm not thinking about the countries exploding
but they're behind us all exploding their forms

the first lesson of 40 is let go
the people you want don't want to stay

what if you lost your gods
or are just finding them again

it is the ides   a day to kill caesars   to betray caesars
a day to fuck caesars
fuck em over   take the throne
it is a day to take the throne

I am taking a mental health day
professors do that   take a day
                    I call myself professor cuz someone else just did
          schools are asylums I told them
I have been dealing with some cases and am a case myself

love rehab Montreal

bloody monster

lust monster wanders
with the thought of a body
rushing bloody thought

blurting out on a
dark bar patio
I think we should stay
getting it on

instantly a man appears
offers his hand
nice to meet you

laugh wild and loud
face blushed
I did not take him up
on his hi

would just bleed
for someone else
all over him

Pepé libido

stayed with a lady
equally alone with her mind
with her flesh

she knew a few of us
league of libidinous
intellectuals

overthinking the body

walked her city of
ancient Catholic repression
of primordial French desire

trying to contain to speak
all that came out of my mouth
was Pepé Le Pew

I should know better
victim of Speedy Gonzales
as I am

but Pepé came forth
I am zee zexzual too-rizt
I am here for zee zex

please tell me ou way
le penis ou way le casbah
oh cheri mwah mwah

mwah mwah mwah
do not attempt to flee
squirm free from my grasp

asses on Rue de Parc

my peripathetic bunny heart
lifted out of my chest
cradled cooed

by a team singing
in honor of a soccer game
or an Olympic contest
an Olympic soccer contest

at the top of lungs
dropping pants
bottoms in the open air

if you don't get a text
from the one you love
love the asses you're with

jousting in Parc du Mont-Royal

we maneuvered
down the stairs on the side
of Royal Mountain

to a congregation
some in full knight attire
channeling horny
into plastic swords

300 years ago
a battle was fought here
at this non-reenactment

this live *Game of Thrones*
a public service
for the young repressed

bodies above below

underneath a cross an angel
beating of the drum
smoking of the herb

sky through wire
permeable metal
stone arm flung upward

about to step into
the circle of the dance
she a concrete ecstasy

thanks Montreal
now I am especially attuned
to French and bodies

I will forget the French

Pandora (the planet in *Avatar*) as my vulva

it's mostly forest and
there are mushrooms in it

some are portobello
some psychedelic

some just random unknowns
that might not sit well

it's flora and fauna
and all that shit

a delicate ecosystem
it's in 3-D

and glows in the dark
clitoral bioluminescence

you need special glasses
to really see it

it's held together by roots
so sensitive

they suck you in
at the slightest touch

diagnose and treat
all your maladies

make your whole life
flash before you

they read you
wordless

know you
better than you do

all the things you left in my house

the router
you're in
the fucking air
of this place
wireless
that falls apart
have to reboot
wastes all
my goddamn time

the internet tv
more air
and waste
another fine
black hole
of video
and memory

the book tablet
for my brain
and reading
erudition
general analysis
conversation
literature
I guess
that's good

the humidifier
misty air

I never use
requires
too much
upkeep
for minimal
sputter and
hydration

the bidet
for my ass health
that I only use
occasionally
cuz the water
is cold
also too much
reminder
of how you were
actually
in my ass and
made me laugh
I need to be
mad at you
for fucking ever
and not laugh
at you cold
tickling my ass

all of them
make me
remember you
but fuck you
cuz I know you

don't remember me
in things
I should
unplug them
take out
the batteries
go to one
of those electronic
dumping events
the city has
trash all the gadgets
that replaced
your actual
fucking presence
but I'm poor
not stupid
traumatized
but thrifty
I should have
some principle
as I remember
how you said
I could be bought
you did
and then
returned me

fuck it
I'm still keeping
all the shit

infinite wop

after Biz Markie's "Alone Again" and Jodie Foster in Contact

I will whip out
this stupid loneliness
it will slip
into the spinning rings
the blinding light
the wormhole
of my hip
my neck
my back

I am OK to go
into another
dimension
a vision of
vast idiocy
and solitude
release it
through my
otherly abled limbs

this solo woe
will drop into
the Möbius strip
of my infinite wop
my idiot savant bop
and be transformed

a slowed forgetting
memory broken
and pieced

back together
by beat
body cracked dumb

I will hum
myself into a universe
of unaloneness
and quadruple suns
wind into
never-before-seen
galaxies
while staying in
one spot

chat up
an alien who looks
like my father
and points me
to the single dancers
on the floor
in their own heads
their own bodies
each a cosmos
alone until collision

infinite wop (video instructions)

type in the urls for these two videos:

Jodie—https://youtu.be/scBY3cVyeyA
Biz—https://youtu.be/OebqNsNRBtU

pause Biz at beginning
watch Jodie from beginning
with volume on until :30
pause and mute Jodie
play Biz
restart Jodie right away from :30 in
and watch
when song is done
unmute or raise volume in Jodie
and close Biz window
watch end of Jodie

Cha Cha DiGregorio lives

evil Danny Zuko draws me out
      black dress flowered   deceptive
            turquoise ruffle rage
     icy flamenca
          swarthy
               to be discarded

yet while I'm here I will devour
                demonstrate
         tame a loose planet
   chop swoop
              scoop Sandy's man
     in the orbit of my skirt

I straddle and am straddled
          I grind and am ground
   two step and twerk
panties décolletage flashed
         dark 'fro and to
             to and fro

I have lived to
      give the blonde some tips
        when she gets Danny back
     she goes bad
       curls black like me
leather dipped
        aware of hips
     the trajectory they offer
   to aimless bad boys

assjet majestic

for ndlela nkobi

at the castle of spa
the greatest of the pool jets
is the throne upon which you
rest your ass

assjet

it shoots from a hole
on the floor of the pool
aims for the corners of you

the perineum jet
taint jet
a massage few
if any are willing to give

I have stalked many
an old Korean lady
for the corner assjet
all the wise elders know
which pool jets work best

assjet is
accompanied by foot jets
that shoot from the back-wall bottom
if you get it right you can float
      on the mushroom
        of the assjet
          spring
get your feet worked as well

at times
the castle is teeming
with masses
and I must begin at the bottom
I must settle for the last assjet

there are three
other water thrones
for the ladies-in-waiting

the assjet assistants
hit the button to activate
the floating seat of power

I am willing
to work my way up to
the most potent
corner jet
outmaneuver outlast
any prior keeper of the seat

it is a holy position
also regal
arms propped on the wall
bum
on
the
water sprout
            legs
            taut
          active
      feet flexed

Queen of Assjet
perched on the corner throne

I observe the masses
righteously
benevolently
it is a relaxed fruitful reign

I stay decreeing
but no one hears me
over the bubbles

at the uptown marsh

We sat by the water and discussed the gull action.
We took a bench. Someone sat on the rocks.
It wasn't me as you thought it might be.
We watched the window washers on the building above the cliff.
They were teetering on their scaffold, one side up, one side down.
They seemed to adjust the platform, even themselves.
We resumed the bird play-by-play. Some beef with a black swan.
I tried to nap on a bacon and chocolate lunch. Got up to a real chest pain.
Returned the gaze to the window washers, lopsided again, more than before.
I thought I should call 9-1-1. A passerby heard my alarm and stopped.
The window washers corrected their perch.
Crisis averted, passerby said, finally passing by.

one nail takes out another

me dicen un clavo saca el otro
all I have seen is one nail
dig the previous one further in

is that how it worked for Christ
were the nails in his hands
replaced by the idea of his father

un dios saca el otro
new god buries
old god deeper

did the saying come about
before the hammer claw
promised to extract false belief

upon excavation
nail upon nail god upon god
withdrawn

an opening

on the lake today

black fly
small rain
green gray

hard to write
with an umbrella
in one arm

you're my real true
boyfriend,
lake

my real love

you move
and I don't wonder
where you've gone

here
and not here
how I like them

those spouses
canoeing
in the rain

places love me
more than people

I love places
more than people

I'm of a place
many

I'm of those
streets
those trees

no but really
this is ridiculous
it is so holy

how the word is made
is how it is all made

all patterns
ripples a lattice
trees and their lines

the surprise of wings

mist like smoke
coming off
the mountains

circles of drops
in the water

it's all gone
all erased
him not loving me

no matter
only this matter
solid earth and sea

my-kus

bitter

fucks up the pitch
all the notes sour
singer witch
let it go

I get involved

in wars of attrition
no one gives up but no one wins
on occasion there is a wicked ecstasy

seducer of hermits

has to retreat to her own cave
will have to coax her out now

gentry caffeine I

I am at a fork
between hills heights there is light
glass an opening

At a nook I want no one to know about. It's already
gentrified, don't want anymore. That is the way with that, it
can't be stopped. Can only catch it in a quiet moment before
the swarm, in the middle of it. Can't control the movement of
this city, only my own. Movement, discovery, the shape of a
moment, a shape someone laid out before me that I am here
to reshape.

have been so grateful
spiritual of late feel like
I have to quit it

In yoga today I was hating people. It might have been
my lack of water or caffeine or both. I won't blame the graceless
man in front of me or the older lady next to me whose mat was
encroaching on mine.

I will blame me or
I will look at me it might
be me who should shift

Brought here by a woman I knew in class. She reminded
me I was almost her teacher. She is my age. When teaching
works, I meet students in all walks, students who can walk with
me. I am a teacher and not. They are the teacher. I get drained.
I need them to think, speak, replenish the conversation. It can't

just be me. If it is I am doing something wrong. I am stirring this iced tea at Gentrifier Café. It's awfully good. Glad it was a local who led me to this place that seduces as it destroys.

how will we move to
avoid destruction what do
we do to remain

Someone comes to take my place. Maybe they can have it. Maybe I'm done with it. Maybe I couldn't resee it as they did. If they take it, I might have to look at me. This place asks you to resee all the time. To walk a street a million times and find a new entry. Like a video game where if you don't grab a key or strike a block or make some particular move you won't get a secret gate to open.

in a place I have been
yet never seen
a student of reseeing

it was the year of the erupting tenements

It was the year of the erupting tenements,
of getting used to nothing,
of feeling lucky that it wasn't us the city ate.
Uptown and down, the indigenous
were caught in the rubble.
The phantom residents of
the instant glass towers above
were revealed and no one blinked.
Their decentralized funds erased us,
made us Dubai and Kuala Lumpur,
Kuala Dubai, gleaming and vacant.
Our rents moved to the
vigesimal system of the ancient Maya.
We were hired to play versions
of ourselves like Hawaiians,
in graffiti grass skirts dancing for Cronuts™.
My one true hero was
the mummy Buddha monk of Ulaanbaatar,
stiff but alive, dusty in his rainbow body.
I invoked him every time
a new Brooklyn asshole
decided I wasn't from there.
I shut down cross-legged,
radiated anti-authenticity,
my skin cells flaking as the asshole tried
to move me to a gallery for sale.
I let roaming coyotes do the work
of terrorizing the interlopers and the ghost rich.
The MTA pitched in with their expertise
in disorientation and abandonment.

I decided on a meeting spot
for after the temples fell,
in the uptown forests
of Inwood and Van Cortlandt.
Telepathically, I texted
the GPS coordinates to my friends,
included a map of secret bike trails there.

bike-kus

West Side Greenway

on the highway,
I covet the bike path—
on the path, I crave river

hit the button blind
like Nazca lines, using an
eye outside of me

genuflecting
at 59th I enter
the road desolate

yacht calls in my zodiac
actual vessel
I own pedals on

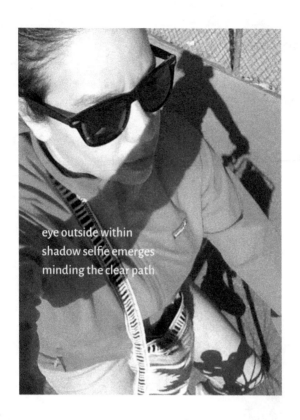

eye outside within
shadow selfie emerges
minding the clear path

Easter Coney (late '80s)

after Christ is risen

the flock moves to the rides seaside
        dressed in their resurrection best

    white engineer overalls and caps
with pink and blue pinstripes

        ruffles on socks and pastel leather
      tilt-a-whirl blurring

  a chill sets in on a candy cloud

      our lord joins the fashion masses
        for technicolor sunset

the safety bar comes down

       he holds on in cold neon
     screaming on the breezes

he the fish he the lamb on the rabbit isle
      Easter conejo
           Conyne Eylandt
    Koni Ailan
        Easter Island

    mutable man on mutable land
  celebrating with his outlaw peoples

in their ketchuped slacks
      sand scuffing shoe shine

  delirious machines spitting

          above oily wooden slats
      before the grimy water

in front of the Himalaya
      the lamb comes down for his crown

      sliding outside the ride
to the selector of the spinning chairs

      the fish clutches his cap
              gets slippery

leaving Coney

ahora sí que no me hallo
am barely conscious for this
the crying has stopped
I got a few things done
was my niece's packing coach
bought some boxes for Ma
after I hugged her at one point
she said I would age fast
cuz I am so sentimental
I told her I stay unemployed
that keeps me young
the tears make you sleepy
that is the only way
I get any rest
damn the phantom
capitalist hand
making this happen
all the blame
on the family is past
at least for moments
I am not right anywhere
was always displacement girl
forever from
the edge of the sea
blood moving now
to the outer banks
of this island
where our people from
the middle of the world
are pushed

it is most home
when I am most decentered
decentral America
unstable a sliver
how do we hold on
to the continent
how do we not fall
into the water

first day ever in Teguz, capital of the homeland
(March 23 2012)

I used to care. I used to sleep.
I used to wonder what it would be like to work in Honduras.
Now I know it is hot and draining instead of cold and draining like New York.
I will always remember standing in front of students in a classroom in Tegucigalpa.
Growing up, a million people asked me what the capital of Honduras is.
I remember my family's country being a joke.
I remember not knowing how to feel about that.
I remember my mother always, we share the same mind.
While I'm far away, I remember my loved ones, they haunt my sleep.
I walk in a dream the further I am from them.
I remember being in New York where I know so many people
and still never seeing anyone I love in a given week.
I remember how I used to get so hurt. Now I just get tired.
I remember the feeling in these students' words, the surprise, the joy.
I am glad to replace my memories with theirs.

gentry caffeine II

the scaffold is gone
can't wait to be here
when it's warmer
when I get off my bike
and can grab a seat
on the bench
and feel the sun
not blocked anymore
and suck on
my iced coffee and
fly off this cliff
that is 181st Street
and be free and poor
and alone but flying
no worry about
having no job or man
or kid or expectation
or ambition
just flying forgetting
the sun hitting
my shoulders
sunglasses
probably should have
my helmet on too
since I have just
a little insurance
the city killing us
as every friend has said
on a train ride yesterday
today losing money

I was hoping for
killing me
the odds so good
for it but even then
they're bad
in this place
of so many people
wanting needing
so much
you have to be that
good or lucky or liked
I get some of that
some times
really needed it now
so I can get
my bike a tune-up
and fly faster
off this cliff
that rock
across the way
is still rotting
so odd and
orange and red
is that rot
do rocks rot
will I rot like that
odd and
orange and red
I am high off the
sheer smell of coffee
bought some
caffeine bags to go
their fancy tea
not a bad price

things not so bad
that I have to
give up fancy tea
but here comes
the sparse summer
hope I have enough
for fancy caffeine
and tune-ups

the sun I can afford

Acknowledgments

Some of these poems have appeared in print in: *The Breakbeat Poets Vol. 4: LatiNext, Bettering American Poetry: Volume 3, Desperate Literature / The Unamuno Author Series Festival: A Bilingual Anthology, Brooklyn Poets Anthology, Shadow of the Geode: The Alternative New Year's Day Spoken Word Extravaganza 2015 Anthology, Like Light: 25 Years of Poetry & Prose by Bright Hill Poets & Writers, Gulf Coast, Ping-Pong, Tribes 15,* and online at *Gulf Coast, Luna Luna, Sensitive Skin, Aster(ix) Journal, Hyperallergic, The Year of the Yellow Butterflies (The Blog), Wordpeace,* and *Black Earth Institute.*

Thank you to all the places that supported my work in the long time between books. They are almost innumerable: Creative Capital, Lower Manhattan Cultural Council, Trust for Governors Island, Northern Manhattan Arts Alliance, Blue Mountain Center, A Gathering of the Tribes, CantoMundo, Word Up Bookstore, CUNY, National Book Foundation, Teachers & Writers Collaborative, Museo del Barrio, Center for Book Arts, Studio 26, School of Visual Arts, U.S. Coast Guard Academy, UT RGV Brownsville, U of Houston, Letras Latinas, Tintero Projects, Unamuno Author Series, Pepatián, BAAD!, The Poetry Project, Desperate Literature, Unnameable Bookstore. I didn't even name all the bars and that is wrong.

Thank you Joe and Wendy Pan Millar of Brooklyn Arts Press for your endless patience, kindness, and friendship.

Thank you to all the people I know and love who make our friendships art. Every one of you is an artist. Thank you for supporting me so many ways. You stay my inspiration, ndlela nkobi, Christopher Myers, Nelly Rosario, Macarena Hernández, David

Aglow, Bakar Wilson, David Pemberton, Stella Padnos, Gabriel García Román, Alba Hernández, Yesenia Montilla, Peggy Robles-Alvarado, Diana Marie Delgado, Ricardo Maldonado, Christina Olivares, Carina del Valle Schorske, Denice Frohman, Lupe Mendez, Jasminne Mendez, Rosebud Ben-Oni, Erika Jo Brown, B.J. Love, Angie Cruz, Emily Raboteau, Matthew Burgess, Melanie Maria Goodreaux, Nikki Johnson, Melissa Fernandez, Mariposa Fernandez, Nestor Pérez Molière, Karin Burrell-Stinson, Denise Burrell-Stinson, Janene Outlaw, Aretha Sarfo, Bruce Morrow, Jeffrey Rosales, Drew Gillings, Jane Gabriels, Elliot Levine. Please forgive me for omitting anyone, if I did, please write your name here _____.

Shout to all the collectives that have brought us ridiculously together: desveladas, bong gay hos, a.k.a. blunt & espinosa, Klub Kitchen, sluts!, sensual (con)sensual, tetas, alto iris, The Unbearables.

Forever thank you to Steve Cannon.

Thank you for giving me your brilliant eyes and thoughts, Lydia Cortés and Joanna Fuhrman.

Thank you for your time and encouragement, Dawn Lundy Martin, Mónica de la Torre, and Urayoán Noel. Truly honored by your words.

Gracias a mi familia, Maldonado, Villatoro, y Cruz. Everyone here and in Honduras. To my niece Emily, who I hope always believes in and nurtures her art, to my brother Waldo, and my mama Vilma, one of the top mamas of all time. To my father, Armando, en el universo, my first great encourager. I am the luckiest to have had you all. Los quiero mucho. El gato, Link, tambien, claro.

May we all make it through this insane time on this planet. Much love and thank you all for having crossed my earthly path.

About the Author

Sheila Maldonado is the author of the poetry collection *one-bedroom solo* (A Gathering of the Tribes / Fly by Night Press). She is a CantoMundo Fellow and Creative Capital awardee as part of desveladas, a visual writing collective. She teaches English for the City University of New York. She was born in Brooklyn, raised in Coney Island, the daughter of Armando and Vilma of El Progreso, Yoro, Honduras. She lives in El Alto Manhattan.

CPSIA information can be obtained
at www.ICGtesting.com
Printed in the USA
FSHW011630110221
78458FS